14

a

Text © 1978 The Estate of Annie M.G. Schmidt
Illustrations © 2011 Sieb Posthuma
English language translation © 2011 David Colmer

Original title: Een vijver vol inkt
First published 2011 in Amsterdam, The Netherlands by
Em. Querido Uitgeverij B. V.

This edition published in 2014 in the United States of America by
Eerdmans Books for Young Readers,
an imprint of Wm. B. Eerdmans Publishing Co.
2140 Oak Industrial Dr. NE, Grand Rapids, Michigan 49505
P.O. Box 163, Cambridge CB3 9PU U.K.

www.eerdmans.com/youngreaders

Manufactured at Tien Wah Press
in Malaysia in October 2013, first printing

20 19 18 17 16 15 14   9 8 7 6 5 4 3 2 1

Library of Congress Cataloging-in-Publication Data

Schmidt, Annie M. G.
[Een vijver vol inkt. English]
A pond full of ink / By Annie M. G. Schmidt ; Illustrated by Sieb Posthuma ;
translated by David Colmer.
pages cm.
Originally published in Dutch with the title Een vijver vol inkt.
Summary: This delightfully humorous collection of poems offers children and the
young at heart a refreshing, inventive look at the world from the well-known
Dutch author, Annie Schmidt. Ordinary events and places become extraordinary
adventures full of imagination.
ISBN 978-0-8028-5433-9
1. Children's poetry, Dutch — Translations into English. I. Posthuma, Sieb, illustrator.
II. Colmer, David, 1960- translator. III. Title.
PT5868.S313E313 2014
839.31'164 — dc23
2013030888

The illustrations were created using drawing and collage.
The display and text type was set in Serifa.

The publication of this book has been made possible with the
financial support of the Dutch Foundation for Literature.

The illustrator received a grant for this work from the
Netherlands Foundation for Visual Arts, Design and Architecture (Fonds BKVB).

FSC
www.fsc.org
MIX
Paper from
responsible sources
FSC® C012700

A Pond
Full of Ink

Poems by Annie M. G. Schmidt

Illustrated by Sieb Posthuma

Translated by David Colmer

Eerdmans Books for Young Readers

Grand Rapids, Michigan • Cambridge, U.K.

The Man Who Writes Fairy Tales

A fairy tale author I know
starts work every day when the roosters crow.

He writes very quickly, he writes without hitches
about fairies and elves and hobgoblins and witches.

He writes about princesses, princes, and kings,
and keeps going till six when the dinner bell rings.

The next morning he's back when the sky's turning blue.
An inkpot's too little, so what does he do?

At the foot of his garden there's a pond full of ink.
The blackbirds all gather around it to drink.

And whenever that writer is at a loose end,
he goes down to that pond to refill his pen.

He's made up ten thousand stories already,
and has plenty more — he's constant and steady.

And if he keeps writing till the day that he dies,
perhaps he'll have written that pond of his dry.

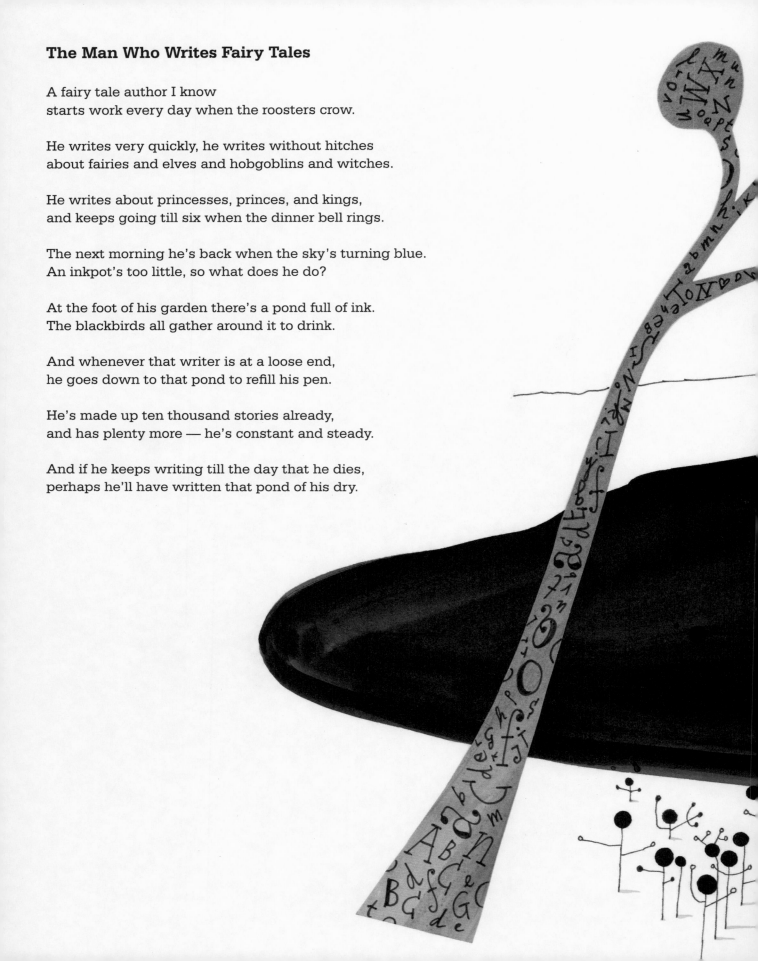

Nice and Naughty

I've had enough! I'm not a lamb!
I don't want to say hello!
I don't want to say "Yes sir, yes ma'am,"
or hear about how big I am . . .
as if I didn't know.
I'll stay out in the yard all day
until I'm sure they've gone away!

I don't want to eat that mushy rice,
I don't want to brush my hair!
I don't want to hear their good advice.
I want to be naughty, not nice,
and lean back on my chair.
And play pirates in the kitchen sink,
and finger-paint with India ink!

And when it rains I'll go and dance
in puddles up to my knees.
I'll stick my tongue out at my aunts,
'cause when I'm old I'll have a chance
to say thank you and please.
And I'll do everything that's wrong,
the whole day long, the whole day long!

I'll make the couch my trampoline
and cover it with grime.
I'll scream and shout hysterically,
and take the dog to bed with me . . .
but I'll say when it's time.
That's all the things I plan to do.
If they don't like it, I'll say "Poo!"

Three Elderly Otters

Three elderly otters longed to go boating
out on the river,
out on the moat.
For years, they had wished they could be
    out there floating,
but, being otters, they couldn't help noting
signs on the seats of every last boat.
Written by renters, the miserable rotters,
they said . . .
FORBIDDEN FOR OTTERS

Three elderly otters standing there crying
there by the river,
there by the moat.
Crying and weeping and finally sighing,
"Maybe the train is fun and worth trying."
But stuck in each window they spied a small note
that had them howling with their heads bowed.
It said . . .
OTTERS NOT ALLOWED

Three elderly otters, tired and spent,
leaving the river
and moat far behind,
saw in a meadow next to a tent
a big row of bicycles ready to rent,
and hung from each handlebar was a small sign
that made their day, and what did it say?
It said . . .
OTTERS DON'T NEED TO PAY

Now the otters ride over the dike,
over the dike and back on their bikes.

The Singing Tea Kettle

Their father's gone out and their mother's gone out,
the children are out and nobody's about,
the kettle's been left on the stove.
Hear it go, hear it go, hear it go: TOOOOT.

The pan full of cabbage says, "Bah, shame on you!
Why must you kick up such a hullabaloo?
I usually couldn't care less,
but you sound like the Orient Express!"

The casserole dish full of gravy and steak
says, "Heavens to Betsy! Give us a break!
There's someone here trying to braise.
I've never braised worse all my days!"

The kettle laments, "It's not me! It's not me!
My whistle's to blame for it all, don't you see?
Whenever I boil, it sings.
I can't stop it doing its thing!"

The parents and children still haven't come back,
the kettle is boiling and blowing its stack.
Its singing is worse than before.
We really can't take any more . . . Can you?

Brian Brink

"Hello, Mrs. Hughes,
have you heard the news?
Brian Brink
from the ice-skating rink
left the tap running in the sink.
It ran for an hour and a quarter.
The kitchen was all under water.
Can you imagine the scene?
He'd just had it cleaned.
Tsk, tsk, tsk."

"Hello, Mrs. Glossop,
have you heard the gossip?
Brian Brink
from the ice-skating rink
left the tap running in the sink.
It ran for a day and a half.
The house was as full as a bath.
Just imagine the mess!
Chairs were floating, no less."

"Hello, Mrs. Gray,
have you heard what they say?
Brian Brink
from the ice-skating rink
left the tap running in the sink.
Six weeks unabated,
the whole street was inundated.
Just imagine the mess!
Cars were floating, no less."

"Hello, Mrs. McMaster,
have you heard 'bout the disaster?
Brian Brink
from the ice-skating rink
left the tap running in the sink.
Five months unabated,
the whole town was inundated.
Just imagine it — five!
No one survived!"

"Look, is that who I think?
Brian Brink from the ice-skating rink?
Brian, you're such a careful chap.
Why'd you leave the tap
running in the sink?"
"Oh," said Brian, "not for long.
The stories they tell are all wrong.
Just a splash, nothing more,
bit of water on the floor
—'bout a cup —
mopped it up,
got it done in a wink,"
said Brian Brink.

With disappointment all around,
the ladies soon were homeward bound.

The Furniture

"Would you like to come out walking?" said the table to the chair,
"I've been standing here forever, and I'd like to take the air."
"Now you mention it, I'd love to come," the chair at once replied.
"Why, we both have legs beneath us that we've never even tried."

"May I keep you company?" the oaken sideboard then inquired.
"Though I am a little heavy and I fear I may get tired.
With these cups and plates and glasses in my chest, I sometimes wheeze.
Would you care to join us, bookcase?" And the bookcase said, "Yes, please."

So the furniture went strolling for an hour on the shore.
But the clock and lamp weren't able and remained there as before.
In the empty house they grumble that the others shouldn't roam.
But they know that life is like that: those who don't have legs stay home.

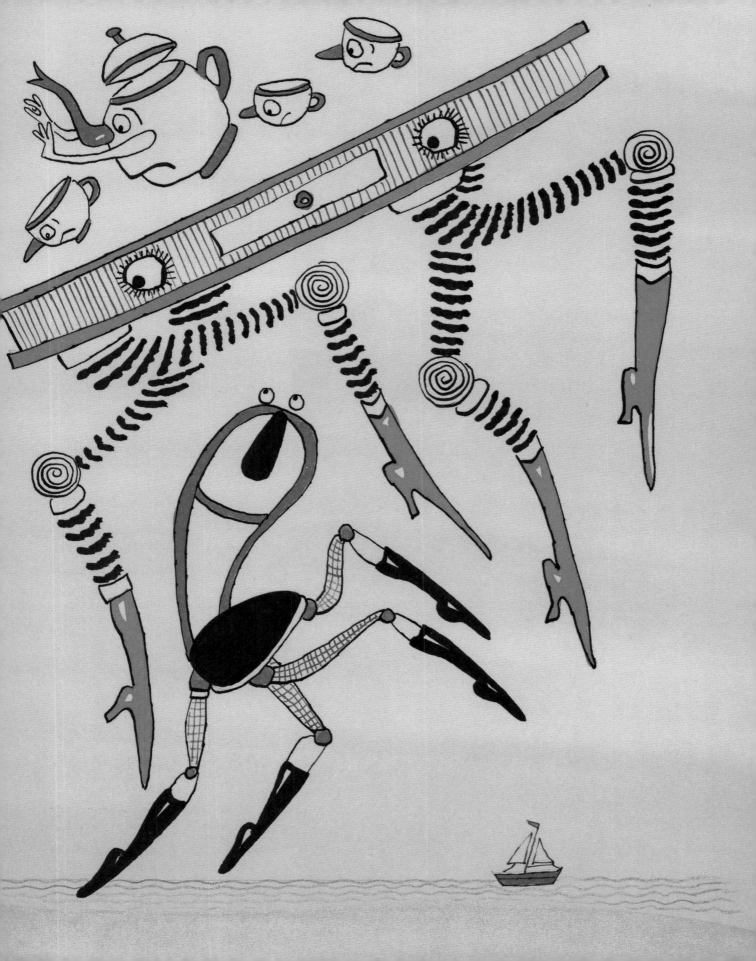

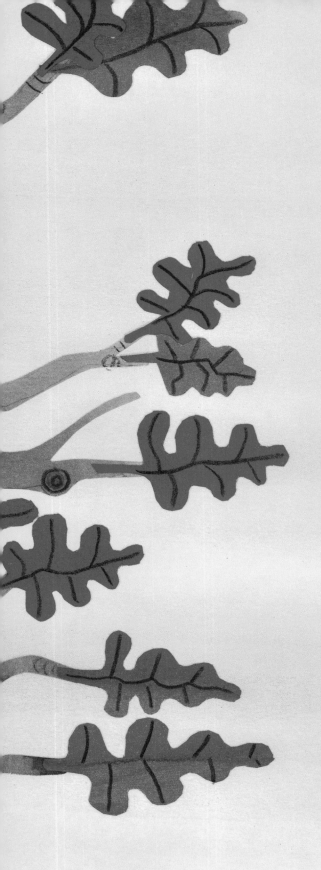

Aunt Sue and Uncle Steve

My Uncle Steve, a charming bloke,
lives up a tree, a big old oak,
he's been there now for ages.
He and Aunt Sue, who's charming too,
just built a floor with boards and glue,
and then moved in . . . in stages.

They sleep up there and eat up there,
it's very cozy, in the air,
except when storms are blowing.
It's quiet, large, and very green,
but Aunt Sue isn't really keen —
she hates a house that's growing.

She's never really worked out how
to park a stroller on a bough.
It leaves her very troubled.
And now the kids are getting big,
she's scared they'll slip on leaf or twig,
and all her fears have doubled.

She'd rather have a lower tree,
but Uncle Steve says, "Goodness me,
we've got it all so pretty.
The kids just love to climb up high.
It's gorgeous sitting in the sky.
Next thing you'll miss the city.

"You say it's like a big birdcage?
These open views are all the rage!
You know I don't like bragging,
but you and I have seen the rest,
and our nest here's by far the best.
Why are you always nagging?"

There wasn't much Aunt Sue could say,
she makes her home there to this day —
it's cozy, if quite humble.
My Uncle Steve's a loving spouse,
the children climb around the house,
and no one takes a tumble.

Isabella Caramella

Isabella
Caramella
has to wash her baby's hair.
Isabella
Caramella
has a cuddly teddy bear
and a cuddly brown gorilla and a green-and-red checked rabbit
and she's got a crocodile — his name is Crabbit.
Isabella
Caramella
plays so sweetly in the sand.
Isabella
Caramella,
with a flower in her hand.
But if someone comes to visit and they happen to be vile,
she stops her game and whispers to her crocodile.
And her crocodile Crabbit
could do with some more lunch,
so he eats the nasty people up: CRUNCH, CRUNCH, MUNCH!
Like Mrs. Hudson-Rote, who thought that children were a pest,
and the lady with the fox-fur stole, who was awfully overdressed.
And the croc eats Mr. Bowen, who had simply got its goat,
down to the nasty last torn pieces of his nasty orange coat.
"Isabella
Caramella,
where is Mrs. Hudson-Rote?
Did you perhaps
see Mr. Bowen
in his orange tartan coat?
Can you tell me why that woman would have left without her shoe?"
Isabella
Caramella
doesn't have a clue.
And she sits there
playing sweetly
with her green-and-red checked rabbit,
and there beside her

in the garden
sits the crocodile Crabbit.
Isabella
Caramella
says, "That was that!" and "There!"
Isabella
Caramella
has to wash her baby's hair.

Are you joking, Mrs. Keller?

"Are you joking, Mrs. Keller?
Keeping bears down in your cellar?
Keeping bears here on a residential street?
If they were rabbits I'd ignore them
and pretend I never saw them,
but these are bears with teeth and claws
    and hairy feet!"

"Mr. Reeves, now just you listen,
I don't need to ask permission.
I'm sure my bears are quite within the law.
Go and check them if you'd rather,
but I got them from my father
and I love them from their ears down
    to their paws."

"Well, in such a situation,
I must go down to the station.
The police will know exactly what to do!"
"Mr. Reeves, you'd better listen,
because if that's a firm decision,
I might need to set my seven bears on you!"

"They are growling. Can you hear them?
You can't miss it when you're near them."
Grrr! Grrr! Grrr! Grrr! Rowl! Rowl! Grrr!
"Mr. Reeves, now that you've listened,
are you sure of your position?"
"Um, not really, Mrs. Keller, maybe not . . ."

"Well, I'll be going, Mrs. Keller,
I'll just pick up my umbrella,
and I hope you have a great time with your bears."
"Oh, Mr. Reeves, you needn't worry,
but I see you're in a hurry,
so, good-bye, and do be careful on the stairs."
    Grrrrrr!

Belinda Hated Getting Clean . . .

Belinda Beronda, from somewhere near Flushing,
was not keen on washing and not fond of brushing.
She was an inveterate cleanliness-hater,
and always postponed her baths until later.
Her bodily odor grew stronger and stronger,
and her hair and her nails grew longer and longer.
Belinda was filthy, a terrible fright.
She looked like a pig, a horrible sight.
And when her mother finally came home
with soap and shampoo and a brush and a comb,
Belinda just started to yell, howl, and glower,
as if she was going to drown in the shower.
Her mother — by now at the end of her tether —
gave in and shouted, "Stay dirty forever!
But if that's what you want, you just walk out that door,
and I won't be your mother anymore!"
So that filthy little Belinda Beronda
took off up the street and started to wander
the highways and byways all over the land,
getting grubby and covered with mud, dirt, and sand,
with grimy smudges all over her face.
The more she avoided a bathroom or scrubbery,
the more she began to resemble some shrubbery.
Grass started growing on her shoes and her clothes,
it covered one leg, then slowly rose,
until she was totally, thoroughly hid
and no one could see that she was a kid!
And then the roots grew into the ground,
and fixed her in place like a tree on a mound.
Birds came and built little nests on her sleeves,
and slowly she grew her own branches and leaves.
A nightmare, but true — you can take it from me —
Belinda Beronda turned into a tree.

So now you know: little cleanliness-haters
end up as trees . . . sooner or later.

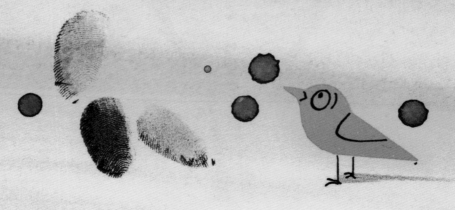

Aunty Jo

When Aunty Jo of Camden Town
came downstairs in her dressing gown
at half past six one morning,
she got an awfully large surprise,
and stopped and stared and rubbed her eyes.
It made her quit her yawning!

She felt like flopping on the chair,
but couldn't 'cause a deer was there.
She yelled and shouted, "Psst!" and "Shoo!"
and grabbed a plate, which she then threw.
The deer just looked up blinking

and listened to the radio,
while poor, unhappy Aunty Jo
was desperately thinking,
and feeling sad and awful weird,
for on the sofa sat a deer.

She wasn't scared, she stood her ground,
but wisely called the city pound
and local health inspector.
The people came from near and far
and looked and shouted, "Ooh!" and "Ah!"
and offered to protect her.

"Well strike me dead," said Uncle Fred,
"The sofa's now a reindeer bed!"
Though no one had the slightest clue
of what to say or what to do,
the deer seemed most contented

and sat so still that Aunty Jo,
who'd longed to have it up and go,
quite suddenly relented.
She let it stay, and in the end
the deer became a dear, dear friend,
who Jo loves like a brother.

And now she uses all its prongs
to hang her ladles, pots, and tongs —
a pan rack like no other.
And Aunty Jo says, "Wonderful!
It's even good for winding wool.
I never lose a spoon or knife,
and the deer now has a goal in life."

The Robbers and the Moon

There were three greedy robbers who had made a cave their base.
It wasn't fun to live there, it was more a storage place,
with boxes full of diamonds and with cases full of gold,
with silver, rugs, and tapestries — though they were flecked with mold.
Those robbers weren't contented, no, their lives were not ideal.
They longed to go out robbing, but there was nothing left to steal.
They scratched their heads and racked their brains, "Ain't there nothin' we forgot?"
But when they looked around them, they could see they'd robbed the lot.

The cave was dark and gloomy, but the moon shone through a chink,
a shining perfect silver moon. That made the robbers think . . .
The moon! Why hadn't they thought of that before? They'd steal the moon!
They'd go and get it straightaway and not a night too soon.
They started stealing steeples, 'cause they're always nice and high,
and when they had three of the things, they thought they'd have a try.
They stacked the steeples one on one and climbed like three baboons . . .
Those robbers were determined that, that night, they'd steal the moon.

Two robbers closed their eyes because they'd started to feel dizzy.
The third one shouted "Cowards!" and climbed higher in a tizzy.
He grabbed the moon and pulled it down, waving to his friends.
They shouted "Careful! Hold it tight!" and he started to descend.
The moon was smooth and slippery and it weighed about a ton.
It slipped right through his fingers, there was nothing to be done!
The moon fell like a lead balloon. They listened for a crash,
but it came down in the river, and they heard a mighty splash.
With one last hiss: hiss-SISS! It sank for all eternity.
Which makes it fair to say, the moon was clearly *hiss*tory.

I'm glad to say there is a group (I don't know if you know this)
of very old professors, a commission, and its name is
The Grand Commission for the Moon and All Things Lunar.
They looked up and saw that it was gone. They should have noticed sooner!

"The moon's not there!" they cried. "It isn't hanging on its hook.
No moon! That's terrible. Just think how stupid we'll look!"
Luckily the chairman had an old moon under his bed.
So quickly they decided to hang that one up instead.

The robbers crept into their cave, their plans in disarray.
They're scared to come back out again and sit there to this day.
And now you know the truth of it. The moon you see up there
is not the real moon after all. It's really just a spare.